THE CALYDONIAN BOAR

MONSTERS OF MYTHOLOGY

25 VOLUMES

Hellenic

Amycus
Anteus
The Calydonian Boar
Cerberus
Chimaera
The Cyclopes
The Dragon of Boeotia
The Furies
Geryon
Harpalyce
Hecate
The Hydra
Ladon
Medusa
The Minotaur
The Nemean Lion
Procrustes
Scylla and Charybdis
The Sirens
The Spear-birds
The Sphinx

Norse

Fafnir
Fenris

Celtic

Drabne of Dole
Pig's Ploughman

MONSTERS OF MYTHOLOGY

THE CALYDONIAN BOAR

Bernard Evslin

CHELSEA HOUSE PUBLISHERS

New York Philadelphia

1989

EDITOR
Remmel Nunn

ART DIRECTOR
Maria Epes

PICTURE RESEARCHER
Susan Quist

SENIOR DESIGNER
Marjorie Zaum

EDITORIAL ASSISTANT
Mark Rifkin

3 5 7 9 8 6 4 2

LIBRARY OF CONGRESS
Library of Congress Cataloging in Publication Data

Evslin, Bernard.
The Calydonian boar / Bernard Evslin.
p. cm. — (Monsters of mythology)
Summary: Recounts the myth of the monster created by Artemis and slain by Meleager and Atalanta.
ISBN 1-55546-242-1
0-7910-0339-6 (pbk.)
1. Calydonian boar (Greek mythology)—Juvenile literature.
[1. Calydonian boar (Greek mythology) 2. Mythology, Greek.]
I. Title. II. Series: Evslin, Bernard. Monsters of mythology.
BL820.C15E96 1989
398.2'454—dc19 88-21789 CIP AC

Printed in Singapore

For a lovely, dreamy huntress
named PAMELA — who also
had trouble with her father

Characters

Monsters

The Calydonian boar (KAHL ih DOH nee uhn)	A giant wild hog, handmade by Artemis

Gods

Zeus (ZOOS)	King of the Gods
Artemis (AHR tuh mihs)	Moon goddess, Goddess of the Chase, Lady of the Silver Bow
Apollo (uh PAHL oh)	Artemis's brother, the sun-god, God of Music and Medicine
Ares (AIR eez)	God of War
Atropos (AT roh pohs)	Eldest of the Fates, Lady of the Shears
Charon (KAHR uhn)	Giant ill-natured boatman who ferries the souls of the dead across the River Styx

Mortals

Atalanta (at uh LAN tuh)	Princess of Arcadia, a huntress
Meleager (mehl ee AY juhr)	Prince of Calydon, a hero

Clymene (KLYM eh nee)	Queen of Arcadia, Atalanta's mother
Iasos (EYE ah suhs)	King of Arcadia, Atalanta's father
Althea (al THEE uh)	Queen of Calydon, Meleager's mother
Oeneus (EE noos)	King of Calydon, Meleager's father
Plexippus (pleck SIH puhs)	Meleager's uncle, Althea's brother
Lampon (LAMP ahn)	Plexippus's and Althea's brother
A shepherd	
A robber band	
Pirates	
Assorted kings, heroes, and warriors who join the hunt	

Animals

Alcon (AL kohn)	The simba hound
The bear	Atalanta's bear brother, a cub grown into a killer
Mother Bear	
Various other dogs, horses, bears, and wolves	

Contents

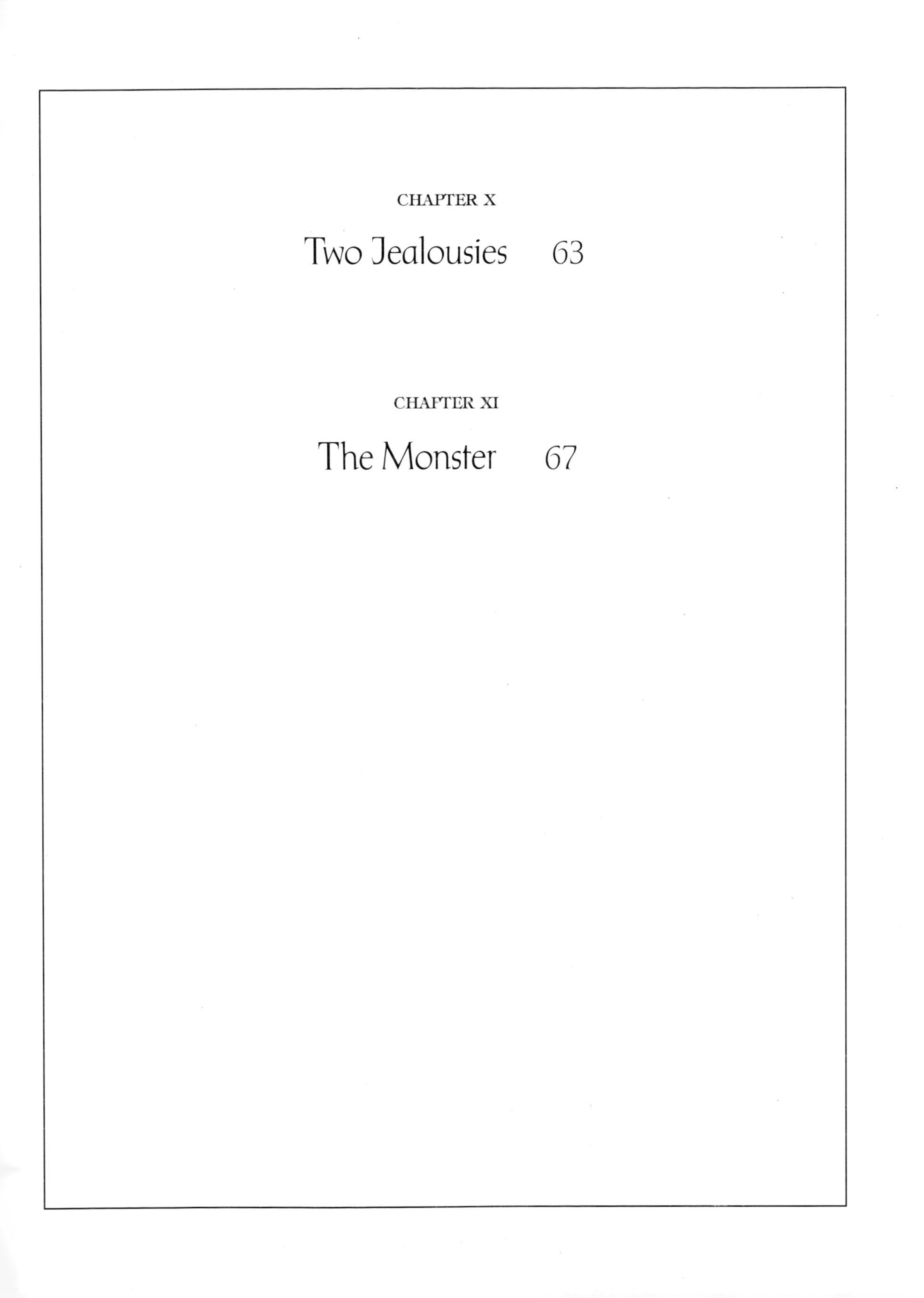

1

Birth of the Boar

arch wind whistled through the trees. Pine needles clashed softly. Epaulets of snow were melting off the high shoulders of Olympus. But in the Garden of the Gods it was always May; the air was scented always with summer flowers, cooled by the rumor of snow.

The gods had dined and were lounging about, gossiping. The talk turned to sport and how they had entertained themselves during the winter, tormenting humankind. This led to a discussion of monsters. Now the gods and goddesses began boasting furiously.

Some time before, Zeus, alarmed by the shrinkage of his human herds, had passed a law, limiting each god to a kill-bag of six humans a month. But the High Ones had found a way to evade this law. They employed monsters. Poseidon bragged of a sea serpent that could flail a fishing fleet to splinters in the space of an hour, and devour all the crews. Hera spoke smugly of her three-bodied giant, Geryon, and of the hundred-headed Hydra whom it was useless to decapitate because for every head cut off two sprang in its place. Athena spoke of the once-lovely sea nymph, Medusa, whose hair she had turned to living snakes, making her into a sight so frightful that anyone looking at her turned to stone. Hades, who was on one of his rare visits to the upper world, told of his hell-hags, the brass-winged, brass-clawed Harpies, and of Cerberus, the three-headed dog who guarded the gates of the Land Beyond Death.

Apollo, the sun-god, who had been listening quietly, noticed that his twin sister, Artemis, Goddess of the Moon, was growing sullen. "What's the matter?" he murmured.

"Come away," she whispered, and led him among the roses. "I can't stand those old braggarts!" she cried. "It's disgusting when they begin yammering about their dreadful pets."

"I know what's really bothering you," said Apollo, who understood his sister perfectly. "You're angry because you have no monster of your own."

"Since you're so understanding of my needs, dear brother, give me some advice. What shall I do?"

"Obviously, there is only one thing to do. Get yourself a monster of your very own."

"The trouble is, Apollo, I loathe and despise the creatures I've been hearing about. I love animals, as you know, beasts of forest and birds of air. Hawk and hummingbird, stag and wolf. I love some for fleetness, others for ferocity, and all for grace and strength. For their natural beauty, in fact. But these slithery sea serpents and fire-breathing dragons, these hundred-headed reptiles and three-bodied giants—no, not for me. Too freakish, too ugly."

"You're hard to please, Sister mine."

"Always have been," said Artemis.

"Well if you don't fancy any of the huge assortment of monsters now available, then you must make your own."

"How do I do that?"

"Oh, you must ask someone more bloodthirsty than I. I am God of Music and Medicine, you know, and must preserve my reputation for gentleness."

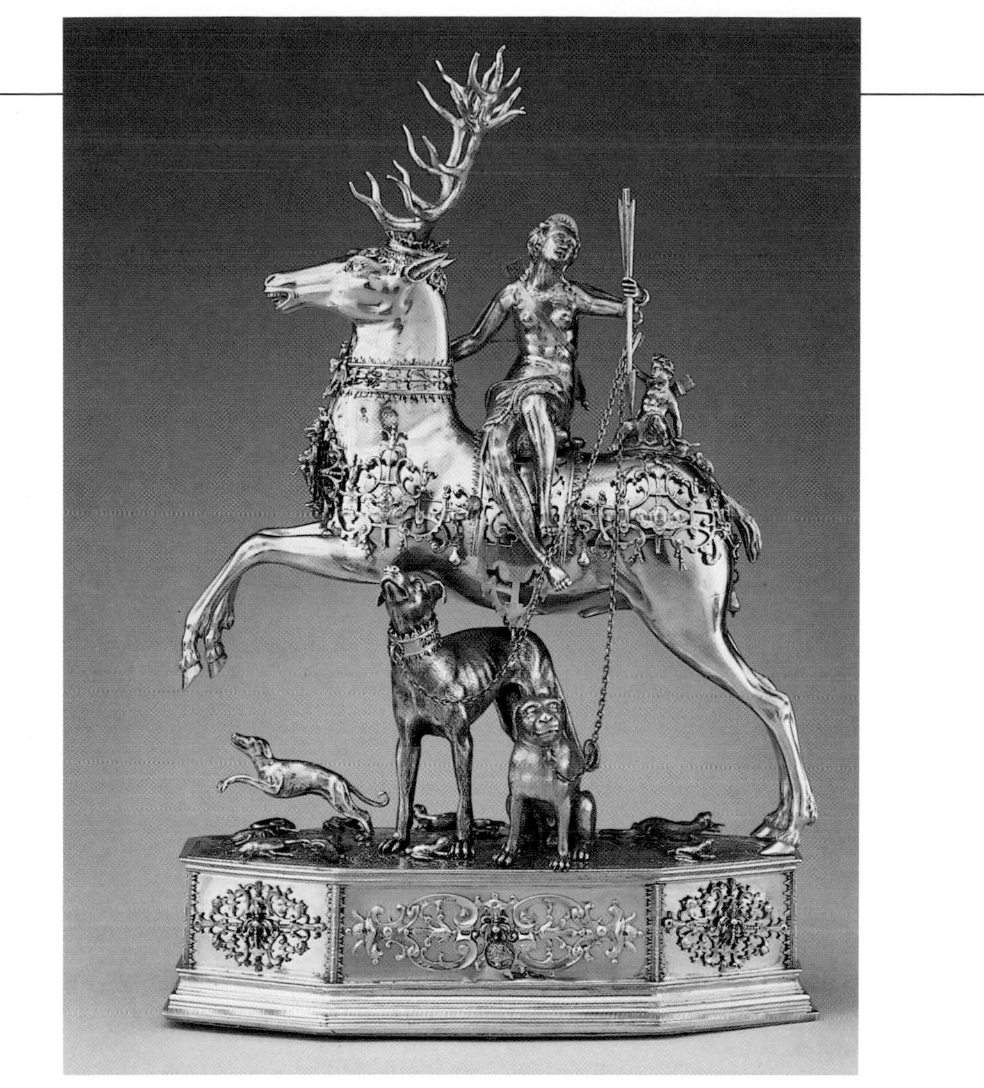

"I love animals . . . for grace and strength.
For their natural beauty, in fact."

Artemis smiled to herself, for she knew how savage her radiant brother could become when angered. She also knew that he would give her no more advice that day, and wandered away from him. She passed near Ares, who was sucking the marrow from two beef bones at once. The bones sticking out of his mouth looked like tusks. And these tusks taken together with his gross snout and poisonous little red eyes made him look like a wild boar.

Artemis drifted up to him and said, "Greetings, kinsman. Have you ever happened to make a monster?"

"I don't need monsters to do my killing for me," growled the God of War.

"Why not? Are you exempt from the game laws?"

"No," said Ares. "As the eldest son of our king, it behooves me to obey his edicts. And I do dutifully limit my personal kills to six per month."

"Do you?" murmured Artemis. "But you are famous for your foul temper, and are surely moved to rage by more than six humans per month."

"Oh yes, Moon. By more than six, or sixty, for that matter. What I do then is simply start a war in the right place. I fan the hot ashes of hatred that reside in the human heart, fan those cinders into flame—either against neighbors or against another tribe, for normal men entertain both kinds of hatred. And when the flame grows huge and red-hot, it is called war. I then take care to move those who have offended me into the worst part of the battle. And lo—those who have angered me are killed, and I am technically innocent of their death."

"Thank you for your courteous explanation, Lord of Battles."

"Nevertheless," said Ares, "I have observed our uncle Hades making monsters when he needed to restaff hell. What he does is take up a handful of vital mud and mold it into any form he desires."

"And where does he get this vital mud?"

"From the River Styx, which borders his dread realm, and is also known as the River of Tears. Over it, vultures hover like gulls. And the winds that blow from shore to shore carry the stench of the roasting pits, the demonic laughter of the torture crews, and shrieks of the tormented. These odors and these sounds sink to the bottom of the River of Tears, and invest its mud with a vicious potence, very good for the making of monsters."

"Thanks again, War," said Artemis, and drifted away, thinking hard.

The moon-chariot driven by Artemis was wrought of silver. Of silver also were the horns and hooves of the six white stags that drew the chariot across the sky, and their eyes were amber. Upon this rainy night, however, the moon was hidden; the goddess rode behind cloud cover.

Down to earth came the silver chariot. Across the meadow and plain it flashed, and through deep valleys, until it reached a chasm called Avernus, which was the gateway to the Land Beyond Death. Here Artemis untethered her stags and let them graze upon the plain. She made herself invisible then, and entered Avernus.

White things they were, seeming now like clouds, now like sheep, now like spouts of steam.

The chasm was really a chain of interlocking caves plunging toward the center of the earth. Down, down, the goddess sped, troubling bats; even invisible, she cast a faint radiance upon the rock walls as she passed. The caves ended in a rocky plain that stretched into darkness. But a river-smelling wind cut through the sulphurous murk. Borne upon the wind also were the curious yearning hopeless cries uttered only by ghosts.

Artemis followed the sound to the shore of a river, which she knew must be the Styx. She heard a strange thwacking sound and saw an enormous creature driving a flock of something before him. White things they were, seeming now like clouds, now like sheep, now like spouts of steam. And she realized they were today's crop of the dead, half-vaporized, flesh still clinging to their bones, memories half-alive in their hearts. She also realized that the one herding them must be Charon, the dread Ferryman, who would take them across the Styx and through the gates of hell.

Charon was a giant. His arms were as big as tree trunks, his hands so broad that he needed no oars to row his heavy boat across the Styx. He simply reached into the water and rowed with his hands. Now, however, he was using those hands cruelly as he drove the whimpering shades toward the dock. Snarling and growling, he swung his tree-trunk arms, beating his flock toward the moored boat.

His hard hands smacking the ghosts sounded like a hundred fishwives softening the bodies of newly caught squid by beating them against rocks.

It was one of the saddest sights on earth, or beneath it, but the moon goddess, watching, was no more moved than we are watching cattle graze on their way to becoming beefsteaks.

She waited until Charon had driven the last of the shades across the pier and into the ferry—watched him dip his enormous hands into the water and begin to row. Watched the boat dwindle and vanish. Then she walked along the shore searching for a

Charon was a giant. His arms were as big as tree trunks, his hands so broad that he needed no oars to row his heavy boat across the Styx.

shallow place. For she did not wish to enter the black water; she needed a place where the shore shelved gradually so that she might kneel upon dry land and dip her hands into the water.

She did finally find such a place, reached into the river, and took a double handful of mud. The water was black, but the mud was a curious reddish brown, and was warm to the touch, seeming to pulse faintly as she watched it. She knew that whatever she molded would come terribly alive in her hands.

She began to shape the mud, working furiously, dipping into the river for more mud, pulling out great gobs of it as the wild beasts took form in her hands. Wolf, bear, panther, each one perfect of its kind, but three times the normal size. She set them on the riverbank to study them. Although she had not yet breathed final life into her creations, the magic mud had translated itself instantly into muscle, sinew, hot blood. The forms waited only for her to awaken them into full, throbbing life.

She couldn't decide which one to keep; they all looked beautiful to her. "I need only one," she said to herself. "And each of these magnificent fierce creatures could serve as my instrument of vengeance, when needed. Let's see then, which of these do I prefer? Shall it be the bear? He's wonderfully big, but bears are sleepy in winter, and my beast must be able to serve the year round. How about the wolf? He's superb, and would be fully alert in all seasons. But wait! Wolves hunt deer—very successfully. A wolf this size might decide to devour the silver-horned stags that draw my moon-chariot. I can't have that. So it will

The magic mud had translated itself instantly into muscle, sinew, hot blood.

have to be the panther. On the other hand, the great cats are even more frantic for live meat than are the wolves. And the deer family is their favorite prey. No, none of these will do. Back to mud they must go.

"What I need is a beast as fierce as these, and as powerful, but one that will kill only people. Is there such a one?"

Artemis pondered. Suddenly the snouted, red-eyed face of Ares gnawing beef bones floated before her. She laughed with joy. "Of course!" she cried. "A wild boar! It can pierce armor with its long, sharp tusks, trample a warrior to bloody rags beneath its razor hooves. And the only animals it kills are hunting dogs that bring it to bay."

She pointed her hands at panther, bear, and bull. They lost shape, became mud, a heap of steaming mud on the riverbank. Artemis dug her hands into it and began to work again. She made an enormous wild boar with tusks like ivory spears and hooves like hatchets.

She stood on the bank of the Styx, admiring it. "Now that I've made this magnificent thing, what shall I do with it?" she murmured to herself. "I'm not yet angry enough at anyone to need an instrument of vengeance. I know! I'll set it down in Africa. There among the lions and apes and crocodiles, it will learn to fight and be ready with its deadly skills when I need them."

She pried open the jaws of the great boar and breathed into it. The mud shape quickened with life. Its red eyes rolled. The goddess leaped onto its back and began to ride it like a horse, urging it into a terrific short-legged gallop, making it go faster and faster. For she was weary of Hades' realm, and wild with eagerness to get back into a drench of sunlight, to breathe air that smelled not of basted sin and ashy tear, but of sea and grass.

2

Give Her to the Mountain

Springtime in Arcadia. Trees were budding, birds singing, flowers opening. Cows were calving; sheep were lambing. It was a happy time; earth and sea rejoiced, and the kindling sky. But all this fertility made King Iasos very uneasy. He summoned his wife, and said:

"If you intend to get pregnant again, my dear, try to produce a son for a change."

"You have something to do with my pregnancies," said the queen. "And why are you belittling our daughters? They're lovely girls."

"Daughters are all right," said the king. "They can be delightful, in fact. But five of them in a row is overdoing it a bit, don't you think? I'll need five large dowries to marry them off to decently powerful princes, and my treasury simply can't stand the strain. What we need this time is a son—who will grow up to be a mighty warrior and help me invade a few neighbors so that we may refill our coffers. I'm counting on you, my queen. Don't let me down."

He was speaking gently, which made the queen shudder. She knew that her husband was never more dangerous than when he was pretending to be gentle. But she concealed her fear, smiled sweetly, and promised to do her best to bear a son.

"Oh, woe," said she to herself when the king had left. "I already feel myself with child again and know that it will be another girl. I don't know how I know, but I do. I also know that he won't keep this one. He'll give her to the mountain, and break my heart."

For in those wicked days, people who did not want their children would take them up the mountain, above the tree line, and abandon them there. Because death by freezing was painless, these parents could pride themselves on taking a lot of extra trouble to spare their child unnecessary suffering. And, to further soften their abominable act, they refused to call it by its right name of *infanticide*, or child murder, but said they were "giving the child to the mountain."

Queen Clymene, however, was very maternal, and resolved that no child of hers would be left to die. She thought and thought, and finally hit upon a plan. "I know what I'll do," she said to herself. "I'll imitate the goddess Rhea, whose husband, Cronos, was devouring her children as fast as she bore them. When her final child, Zeus, was conceived, she concealed her condition until she could conceal it no longer, and only then did she inform her husband that she was with child again. Then she bore it secretly, three months before it was expected, smuggled it out of the palace, and gave it to the mountain nymphs to raise. Then wrapped a stone in swaddling clothes and gave it to her husband, who swallowed it and suffered a major bellyache. Well, I'll do the same thing. I know a pair of kindly, reliable shepherds who will raise the child as their own—especially as I shall pay them well. As for defying my husband this way, I'd do it a hundred times over to save this daughter, whom I already love. What was good enough for the goddess is good enough for me."

The queen kept her secret. The child ripened within her for

three months; only then did she tell her husband what was happening. He frowned and repeated his demand for a son, and she promised to do her best.

Six months later she gave birth to a girl, whom she named Atalanta, and bade a faithful servant take the baby out of the castle and deliver her to the shepherd family. She also sent certain instructions to the shepherds, and a fat bag of gold. Then she told her husband that she had miscarried.

Queen Clymene was very maternal and resolved that no child of hers would be left to die.

But, as has happened to so many parents since, her anxiety for the welfare of her baby was what brought great trouble to the child. For she had overpaid the shepherds. The husband drank himself foolish one night and bragged about his new wealth. No one quite believed him, but the story spread and reached the ears of an outlaw band, who didn't believe the rumor either, but checked it out anyway. Robbery was their trade, and they were very professional.

They caught the shepherd as he was pasturing his sheep, built a small fire of twigs, and grilled the soles of his feet until he told them where the gold was hidden. After they killed him, they went to his cottage, collected the gold, and the new widow, and vanished into the hills.

The child, Atalanta, awoke in the empty cottage and immediately began to call for food. Although only a few months old, she had a loud, bawling cry—which grew louder when no one answered. She cried herself to sleep, finally, and awoke hungrier than ever, and began to howl. No one came.

She swung herself out of her cradle and fell to the floor with a loud thump. But she had a sturdy, rubbery little body, and was unhurt by the fall. She started to crawl. The cottage had only two rooms. She searched both of them, and knew that she was alone. She crawled outside. It was a cloudless morning. The grass was warm. The air smelled of sunlight and pine needles and distant snow. She rolled in the grass, gurgling happily.

She ate some grass and spat it out. She ate a handful of dirt and a few ants, and was not pleased. She craved milk and barley mush. She crawled off to find them.

The eastern slope of a mountain gets the morning sun, but cools off quickly in the late afternoon. The naked baby, still searching for food, was stabbed by a cold wind. She wedged herself into the cleft of a rock that still held heat. She was miserable. Bushes loomed and seemed to grow as she watched them. Hunger clawed her belly. She howled into the blue shadows.

Her cries attracted the attention of a she-bear that was searching the slope for a lost cub. The huge blunt-headed shaggy beast came nosing up to the squalling baby. She didn't know what it was, but it was alive and young and very edible. She came closer.

"The goddess Rhea . . . wrapped a stone in swaddling clothes and gave it to her husband. . ."

Atalanta felt a great vital warmth; she smelled milk. Her hands reached out and grabbed fur. She swung herself up under the bear and began to nuzzle for milk. The she-bear, amazed, felt a tiny mouth upon her. She was shocked by its toothlessness, but knew the sweet easement of milk being drawn from her swollen udders.

Very gently she took the baby in her jaws and began to climb the slope with her swaggering shoulder-rolling walk. She hadn't found her cub, but this thing would do for the moment.

Atalanta felt the great teeth upon her; they seemed as gentle as the arms of the shepherdess. She was not afraid. She rode happily through the cold blue light, up the slope toward the bear's cave.

3

The Wild Child

She-bears produce one or two cubs a year. They begin life as fluffy balls of fur, cute and playful as puppies; within a year, however, they are half-grown, full-grown at two. By the time the child Atalanta was five years old she had wrestled with five different litters of bear cubs, and was as strong and fleet as a little wild animal herself.

She loved to climb rocks, run full tilt down the hills, scramble up trees and ride their branches, race along the beach and swim in the sea. Only one thing troubled her: Why was she so smooth skinned while her brothers and sisters were so nice and furry? She was also different in her refusal to hibernate. When she was very small she had no choice because the mother bear blocked the exit with her huge body, and when Atalanta tried to squeeze past to the mouth of the cave, Mother Bear would simply swing a big paw in her sleep, knocking the child back inside.

But by the time Atalanta was five she had learned to vanish into the woods at the first signs of cold weather and remain outside till spring. When she returned to her family the mother bear, always irritable after hibernation, would cuff her a few times, then roll her over on the ground and lick her tenderly to show

If she wasn't quite a bear, what was she? She sought the answer in other animals. Deer looked smooth. . .

that she still loved her hairless little Atalanta even though she was too wicked to spend the winter sleeping in a cave as all proper bears do.

Atalanta wondered about being so different. It puzzled her mightily. If she wasn't quite a bear, what was she? She sought the answer in other animals. Deer looked smooth, but on closer examination she found that they, too, had fur—short fur, but fur nonetheless. Worms were smooth, but she didn't relish the idea of being related to them. Besides, some worms—caterpillars for instance—were quite furry. She came upon a python one day, and watched him engorge a young doe and then fall asleep while digesting it. She went closer and fearlessly rummaged among the great snake's coils. It was quite smooth. On the other hand it was very unlike her—legless as a worm. And she didn't like its feeding habits. So things were more of a puzzle than ever.

It was early autumn. The sun was still hot, although the night winds had begun to show a sharp edge. Atalanta sat on a warm stone dangling her legs into a stream and gave the big question more thought. How else was she different besides the furlessness? Well, there was the matter of her slow growth. Young cubs that she could hold on her lap were wrestling with her on equal terms by the time of their first hibernation and were much larger by the end of a year. They had become full-grown, powerful beasts by the end of two years, while she seemed to have hardly grown at all.

Perhaps it was because of their habit of sleeping all winter in a cave? This year she might try it herself. And so to the mother bear's delight, Atalanta did not vanish that winter but entered the cave with the others and tried to fall asleep.

She couldn't. It was too stuffy in there. She found it hard to breathe. Nevertheless, she wanted to be like the others, oh, how she wanted to be. She decided on a compromise. She would sleep with her body inside but her head outside. Ah, this was splendid! Her body was warm but her face was nice and cool. She smelled pine and could see the stars.

Just as she was sliding into her first sleep, however, she came suddenly awake. She saw a pair of burning eyes; a foul smell enveloped her. She knew that something was about to eat her face off. Swift as a lizard darting between rocks under the shadow of a hawk, Atalanta slid into the cave and nestled close to the huge hot throbbing body of her mother and realized that her idea had no chance of working. She could not sleep the winter through half inside the cave, half outside, because by spring only the inside part would be left.

Bears did not ask themselves questions.
They were happy to be what they were and nothing else.

At dawn, she slipped outside again, raced down the hill, and dived into the surf. She entered color, was in a cauldron of pink and blue, purple and gold. The sea was very cold but the colors seemed to keep her warm. When she came out her teeth

A small fishing boat had darted out from behind a jutting of rock . . .

were chattering. She raced along the beach as fast as she could—until the sun had climbed a bit and she was warm again.

Then, walking slowly along the beach, watching the sea change, watching it lose its hot colors and become a tilted jade saucer, she kept wondering what to do, since hibernation didn't work. How else could she try to become more like the other bears? How else was she different besides being smooth skinned?

An idea flared. The answer to her question lay in the question itself. For nothing troubled her brothers and sisters. Or full-grown bears either. They did not ask themselves questions. They were what they were, were happy to be what they were and nothing else. Nor did deer or fox or fish, wolf, or python ask themselves questions. To be more like them she would simply have to stop tormenting herself with questions, stop challenging her own existence.

At noon when the sun rode high, she ran into the surf again. Swimming underwater, she could not see that a small fishing boat had darted out from behind a jutting of rock and was casting a dragnet. She was pleased because she knew she had swum farther underwater than she ever had before. But now she needed to breathe. Shooting up toward the surface, she swam right into a net.

Her weight made the mouth of the net close. The fisherman felt his net sagging and pulled it in swiftly. And was amazed to see what he had caught. Then he shouted with joy. For he thought that he had caught a young Nereid. And the legend among fisherfolk was that anyone who landed a young sea nymph and was able to keep her for a year would be ensured a rich crop of fish for the rest of his life.

4

Gain, Loss, and Revenge

Satisfied with his morning's catch, the fisherman sailed for home. The child lay in the bottom of the boat, still wrapped in the net. She kicked and threshed and tried to bite through the mesh, but its cords were tarry and fishy and too strong to cut with her teeth.

The boat sailed into a tiny harbor girded by boulders. The fisherman lifted the net out and carried it to his beach hut, which he had built out of driftwood. He carried Atalanta inside, making her more furious than ever. This was the first time she had ever been in a house, and she hated it. It seemed like a small fishy cave, even more airless than the bears' den.

The man lifted the net onto a stone slab where he scaled fish. In order to deceive him, the girl had stopped struggling and lay very still. He opened the mouth of the net. She sprang out like a little demon and bit his hand savagely, clawed with her fingers, and aimed for his eyes. He shrank back, but she slashed her nails across his face, leaving bloody furrows.

She sprang off the slab and flashed toward the door, and sped down the beach toward the sea. But she heard something that stopped her in mid-stride. It was his voice, calling. It was like nothing she had ever heard, not like birdcall or wolf howl or the grumbling summons of Mother Bear. Those sounds were easy, very simple: "Come." "Hunt." "Eat." "Flee." But the voice of this bitten man held meaning behind its sound and meaning behind its meaning. It was speech, human speech, cleaving its way through her hard head bone to the very center of her thoughts. Identifying her. Creating a magical response. Binding her to the spot.

She turned and waited as the man slogged slowly through the sand. She waited until he came to her. She kept staring at him as he knelt on the beach and stroked her hair with his bleeding hand. She watched his lips move—as if listening with her eyes. She had never heard words before, but half understood them as he spoke.

"Do not run away from me, little sea nymph. Stay with me. I'll be very good to you. I live here alone, all alone. I have no children. My wife was swept overboard in a storm and drowned. And so was our child. You shall be my child, and I shall love you like a daughter. You shall be my Nereid daughter, full of strange powers. You shall go fishing with me and my nets will always be full. And after a year you may leave me again, if you wish. But I shall love you all my life long."

Atalanta dwelt with the fisherman through that winter. She did not miss her bear family. They were asleep in their cave and she wouldn't have been with them anyway. She would have been living by herself in the winter hills. And the fisherman was a man very close to the earth and to the sea, attuned to the movement of animals and of fish. He knew where mullet dwelt, and cod, where lobsters fed, and what lured the octopus. He understood that only a sense of freedom would bind the wild child to him, and he allowed her to do as she pleased.

Although not a man of words, by any means he knew that

she craved to learn human speech. And so he spoke to her. He taught her the meaning of words, and she learned faster than he taught. By springtime she could speak as well as he.

She went fishing with him, and was a great help. For she could swim like a seal, and was able to dive overboard and stay under to free a tangled net. She could even catch fish in her hands, and could skim across mossy, slippery rocks and catch crabs, which he used as bait for octopi.

She told him stories. She told him about how she had lived with bears. And he listened, enraptured. But the meaning of the tales did not sink in, for he still thought she was a Nereid child, and that the tale she was telling was some fragment of ancient undersea lore from time beyond memory when the earth was covered by water and those he knew as land animals dwelt underwater with the fish—wolves and bears, deer and panther and hawk. And the proof of this, he knew, was the seal, which had remained half animal even after the seas had withdrawn from the land.

But fisherman and wild child were fated to part before their year was up.

The robber band that had killed the shepherd who had taken care of the infant Atalanta had now split up. Former seamen, they had decided to return to the sea, but as pirates. They had stolen a ship and begun to prowl the waters. Laden ships

But fisherman and wild child were fated to part before their year was up.

they allowed to pass, and waited till they came home, riding high on the water, for then they knew that the cargoes had been sold and that the ships now carried treasure. These ships they grappled and boarded in the dark of night. Then they cut the throats of their crews, threw the bodies overboard, and helped themselves to the gold.

Normally, they did not bother with fishermen whose only wealth was their daily catch. But, as it happened, they were on the lookout for a small hidden harbor where they could moor safely between voyages. They sailed into that harbor one night, slipped silently into the circle of rocks, moored there, and sneaked ashore. They moved very silently, but Atalanta, who was still unable to sleep indoors, had bedded down beyond the hut. She slept as alertly as a wild animal, and heard something coming.

She sprang into the hut and shook the fisherman awake. "Something's coming," she whispered.

He leaped out of bed, seized his fish spear, and rushed out into the moonlight—and received an arrow full in the throat, and died as he fell.

The pirates rushed into the hut to see if there was anything of value inside. One of them caught Atalanta. While it was not their habit to take prisoners, they sometimes kept a healthy child to sell at a slave auction. Atalanta swept a knife from the scaling table and slashed the hand that held her, cutting its finger tendons. She wrenched herself free and darted out the door. When they chased her outside she had vanished.

But she did not leave. She yearned to be off this bloody beach and into the hills where her bear family would be emerging from their cave. She stayed on the beach, however, keeping herself well hidden, and watched the pirates as they made themselves at home in the fisherman's hut. They enlarged the hut so that they could use it as a headquarters when resting between voyages. She observed their habits. When they sailed out on a raid they always left someone behind. For they returned at night always,

Atalanta waited for a day that promised a cloudy night . . .
and took care to study the man left behind.

and it was the duty of the one left behind to build a signal fire on moonless nights so that the ship could find its way back into the tiny harbor.

A plan ripened in the child's head. Like all wild animals she could read the weather. And she waited for a day that promised a cloudy night. After the ship slipped out of the harbor, she took care to study the man left behind. For he would get his breakfast, she knew, as soon as the ship vanished from sight. And each of the men had different feeding habits. One of them liked berries for his morning meal. Another preferred to catch a fish and roast it on a stick. A third liked to dig up clams and eat them raw. While still another craved honeycombs.

And it mattered to her which one would eat which breakfast. If it was the honey eater she would lie in ambush near a hollow tree where bees hived. If it was the berry eater she would hide among the blackberry bushes. She knew these bushes well, for they provided her own breakfast. She had a bear's taste for berries. Hiding among a fringe of trees, observing the hut, she saw a man come out, carrying a bow and arrow, and knew it was the one who liked to shoot a brace of doves for his meal.

She would have preferred the honey eater or the berry eater. Still, this one was better than the one who dug clams or caught fish, for either of those she would have had to stalk across an empty beach. This one, although carrying a bow with a notched arrow, and alert for sound and movement, would at least have to come among the trees.

She climbed a tree where doves roosted. They flew away as she climbed, but that didn't matter. She could imitate their mourning call. She had kept the scaling knife, and unsheathed it now. The man came among the trees, arrow notched. She cooed like a dove.

He came to the tree and looked up. It was a thick-boled oak tree. She crept around the trunk, moving silently as a squirrel, until she had come around in back of him and was poised above him. Then she leaped.

The man beneath the tree was a huge fellow. She knew that her weight could never bear him down. So she did not jump feet first; she dived upon him, knife held at arm's length, straight in front of her as she dived. And it was the knife that drove into him first, severing his spinal cord. He flopped like a fish on the ground, then was still.

Having been killed so suddenly, and in the midst of such hungry life, his wide-open eyes still seemed to be searching the tree for pigeons. Atalanta left him there. She ran down to the sea to wash the blood off her in a long, cold, cleansing swim. She ran back into the woods, found her berry bushes and had a big breakfast, then went to sleep.

She awoke in the late afternoon. She was restless, full of boiling energy, and she had things to do before nightfall. She walked down the beach for a few miles to where the rocks formed a jagged barrier between land and sea. On the beach were balks of driftwood, very heavy, but not too much for her strength. She dragged together a huge pile of logs.

By the time she had finished, night had fallen, the moonless night she had wanted—solid cloud cover, not a chink for light to shine through.

She ran back to the hut, took a dry branch and thrust it into the fire that always smoldered on the hearth. Then, holding her torch high, ran back to the woodpile. Shadows coursed after her, ran before her, as the windswept flame of her burning stick bent this way and that. And the dancing shadows seemed to rejoice in the vengeance that was to come.

She reached the pile of driftwood and poked her lighted branch among a bunch of dry twigs at the base of the pile. Pine twigs they were, rich in tar. The fire flared. She dragged more driftwood near in case the pirate ship had to stay out so long that she would need to feed the fire again. Then she squatted on the beach and waited.

The wind was light that night, coming in puffs from different directions. It didn't matter. The pirates always dropped sail at night and rowed into the harbor. No, it didn't matter, sail or no sail, wind or no wind. Beyond these jagged rocks the water swirled in a ferocious riptide. Just that afternoon she had seen huge tree trunks caught in the riptide, spinning like chips before being hurled upon the rocks.

She waited, watching the fire, trying to judge whether it was time yet to build it higher. She didn't want to build it too high, for the pirates, professionally suspicious of everything, might become alarmed by too huge a blaze. So she kept the fire as close to the size of a normal signal fire as she could. But she didn't mind this labor. She was being eaten by impatience, and fetching wood passed the time.

Finally, she heard what she had been waiting for: the grinding of wood upon rock, breaking timbers, men screaming. They screamed for a long time. They were all strong swimmers, she knew, but no one could last in that surf.

The screams died to whimpers, then stopped. But she could not leave. She waited on the beach till the sky paled; then she heard other cries, very welcome ones, the shrieks of gulls spotting an early feast. She knew what the gulls were saying, but she had

Beyond these jagged rocks the water swirled in a ferocious riptide.

to see for herself. Nimble as a water rat, she skimmed out on the slippery rocks until she found what she was looking for: the bodies of men sprawled among the jagged boulders. And fat black crabs scuttling away from the white blur of the men's faces, lest they, too, be caught by the diving gulls.

Atalanta was satisfied. Those who had killed her fisherman were dead themselves now. She turned and raced away, off the beach, through the woods, over meadows to the foothill, and up into the mountains where the mother bear was waiting, she knew, for her return. . . . And this year's cubs would be big enough to wrestle.

Que
tal?

5

The Fatal Crones

Those three dire sisters, the Fates, were busily at work. Clotho, the youngest hag, was twirling her spindle, drawing thread from flax. Lachesis, the middle sister, was measuring the thread. And Atropos, eldest of the fatal crones, and their leader, wielded her shears cutting the thread of life, which Clotho had spun and Lachesis measured.

Every time she cut a thread, someone died.

Suddenly, Atropos shrieked. "What's the matter?" cried Lachesis in alarm.

"I'm bored," growled Atropos. "Bored, bored, bored."

"Oh, no," murmured Clotho.

"Oh, yes," cried Atropos. "Things can't go on like this. They must change."

"But we're changeless," said Lachesis.

"We can decree change," said Atropos. "For we are the Deciders. Drop your spindle, Clotho. Lay down your measuring rod, Lachesis. Stop working, both of you, and listen to me."

The younger hags, who always obeyed Atropos in everything, put aside spindle and rod and sat quietly.

"What is so boring," said Atropos, "is that we sit up here

ordaining how everything will come out. Who will live and how long; who will die and how soon. Then, having decided, we watch everything turn out exactly as we planned. Well, that's our duty in the high scheme of things, but I tell you that after ten

"A strong prince has just been born, heir to the Calydonian throne. . ."

thousand years of it I'm bored. And I've decided that even our stern routine can have a little variety. For have not the creatures called mortal been created for our entertainment? Well, let us be like the other gods and give ourselves a little sport with these humans before we kill them off. You ask me how?"

The others nodded in unison, although they had not asked anything.

"Well, I'll tell you," said Atropos. "We'll play with something I've just invented and choose to call *free will*. We'll decide what to do with each life as before, but sometimes we'll pick a certain destiny and put a twist in it. We'll say, 'You shall die young *if* you do this,' or 'You shall live long *unless* you do that,' or the other way around. We won't do this with everyone, of course. Only the strongest mortals can handle free will. So we shall choose some strong, interesting ones and mix some choice into their destinies, and watch them struggle in our net of *ifs* and *unlesses*, trying to decide what to do. And that will entertain us, will it not, Sisters, will it not?"

"Oh, yes," murmured Clotho and Lachesis. "That will surely entertain us."

"Very well. I'm off to Calydon."

"Why Calydon?"

"I have been watching a birth. A strong prince has just been born, heir to the Calydonian throne, and his personality should prove interesting enough to provide us with some sport. His and his mother's, too. I shall go down there now and bestow the treacherous gift of alternatives."

6

A Prince, a Hag, and Two Evil Uncles

lthea, queen of Calydon, lay in the royal bedchamber, reaching her arms to take her newborn infant from the hands of the midwife. She expected to see something red, bald, and squalling, but this one had been born with a black shock of hair. He did not scream or whimper, but uttered a deep chuckling sound.

Then she did hear a scream, but it was the midwife, who was scuttling backward, retreating from something that had appeared in the room without coming through the draped archway. And what the young queen saw was fearsome enough to make anyone scream: a very tall and emaciated crone. Lank white hair fell about the wedge of wrinkles that was her face. And out of that face glared two eyes, blue as the core of flame.

The hag stood there, leaning upon a staff, glaring down at the royal bed. Then she raised her staff and pointed it at the young woman.

"Althea, Queen of Calydon," she growled, "young mother, behold!" She whirled, flinging the staff into the hearth, where it immediately caught fire. "See that stick burning there? When it is consumed by flame, your son shall die."

The queen leaped from the bed with such furious speed that no one would have thought that she had given birth just an hour before. She rushed to the hearth, stuck her hand in the flame and pulled out the charred stick.

"Will my son live?" she cried.

The hag laughed. "*Unless* you return the stick to the flame, or someone else does."

"If I keep it safe, unburned, will he live?"

"If, if, if!" shrieked the hag. And vanished.

The queen had no way of knowing that she had been visited by Atropos, "Lady of the Shears." She did know, however, that whoever the crone was, goddess or demon, she possessed awful powers and had to be believed. Althea, thereupon, took the charred stick in a massive brass chest, had it bound around with heavy chains, and ordered no one to open it on pain of death.

"Now my beautiful baby is safe," she said to herself, "and shall grow into splendid manhood, and become a mighty king."

And she took him into her arms to feed him.

Now, Althea had two brothers who were very wicked. Ever since their sister's marriage to King Oeneus, these men had been plotting to overthrow the king and seize the Calydonian throne for themselves. They pretended to love their younger sister very much. And she, who had a very trusting, passionate nature, believed them and tried to love them in return, although there was something about them she had never liked. But she blamed herself for this, and tried harder than ever to care for them as much as they said they cared for her.

They felt hopeful about their chances of seizing power because they knew they could manipulate the queen. They also thought that their royal brother-in-law would be easy to undermine because he was more interested in the hunt than in ruling. But they were furious when the prince was born, for their favorite

Althea had two brothers who were very wicked.

oracle had warned them that this infant, if allowed to live, would grow up to be a mighty warrior.

The brothers, whose names were Plexippus and Lampon, always met in a certain secret grove when they were plotting. They were extremely suspicious, both of them, and always feared that servants were trying to eavesdrop.

"Well, our course is clear," said Plexippus. "We must see to it that this pesky nephew of ours does *not* grow up to be a mighty warrior."

"What do you mean?" said Lampon.

"What do you think I mean? We'll have to get rid of him."

"How?"

"Well, we can't do much while he's in the nursery. The castle is too closely guarded. We'll have to wait till he gets more active, runs about, and so forth. Then we'll have plenty of opportunities to arrange a little accident."

"Sounds good," said Lampon.

The tiny prince, who was named Meleager, grew into a child, and his mother loved him more than ever. His father, too, was pleased with him. He was different from other children. As soon as he could talk, he demanded weapons, declared his love for dogs and horses, and insisted that his father take him hunting or he would run away and hunt by himself.

The king was delighted to humor his only son. He ordered his smith to make a tiny spear and a bow that shot arrows no larger than darts. These were not toys; they were weapons. Meleager practiced spear handling and archery for hours each day, and became very expert.

The evil uncles had been waiting more or less patiently all this while. But now Plexippus thought it was time to strike. He summoned his brother to the grove.

"Well, Lampon," he said, "the time has come to move against that brat. No doubt you've been spending the years since his birth in planning some brilliant stroke."

"No, I haven't," said Lampon. "I leave the planning to you."

"All of it?"

"Every bit."

"Why?"

"You're smarter."

"Then what is your contribution to our effort?" asked Plexippus.

"I'm braver. And for what we want to do we'll need brains and guts. Me as much as you. So let's hear your plan. I know you have one."

"Yes, I do. Fortunately for us, the foolish king spoils his son in every way possible. Actually allows him to go hunting with the court. He has his own pony, his own dogs, his own special little weapons. Disgusting spectacle. But it serves our purpose. Do you know that dog I just imported from Africa? That simba hound?"

"Call that murderous beast a dog?" cried Lampon. "Looks more like a cross between a wolf and a lion."

"Well, they use them to hunt lions there."

"You'd better get rid of him or we won't have any servants left. He's already killed one dog handler and bitten the arm off another."

"Yes," laughed Plexippus. "Good practice. Now we'll provide him with a royal feast."

"What do you mean?"

"We'll starve him for a few days first, then turn him loose near the king's kennels. He'll prowl about looking for something to eat. The dogs inside will smell a strange dog and begin to howl. They'll make a mighty clamor. And Meleager, who meddles in all kennel matters, will run out to see what's happening. He fancies he can handle any animal, you know. I've heard him bragging about it. And his parents boasting, too. So he'll come out and see this strange, impressive-looking dog and decide it's something he wants for his pack. He'll go up to it, and our hungry simba hound will do the rest. Should be able to finish him off in two bites."

"And I suppose," said Lampon, "that you're expecting me

"The dogs inside will smell a strange dog and begin to howl."

to let that damned brute out of his pen and lead him all the way to the castle? Is that right?"

"Why yes," said his brother. "Now's the time to show some of that bravery you were talking about. I've done the thinking, the next part is up to you. None of our dog handlers will go near him. Nor any of our slaves. They say they'd rather be flogged to death than eaten alive. So now it's up to you. You should be all right if you wear a full suit of armor. Even a simba hound can't bite through brass."

"I'm going to try to develop some brains," said Lampon. "It's getting too dangerous to be brave."

7

The Simba Hound

eleager awoke to the sound of his dogs making a racket such as he had never heard before. Not the baying of hounds following a hot trail, nor the ragged snarling of a pack going in for the kill, but a howling chorus of pure outrage.

He leaped out of bed and rushed from the castle, ran out onto the courtyard and across the flagged stones to the kennel. The dogs' voices changed as they heard him coming. The howls were laced with barking which said: "Let us out! Let us loose!"

The moon swam into a chink in the clouds and he saw what the pack was howling at. A shape loomed near the kennels. The moonlight struck green fire from its eyes. It stood like a dog, but larger than any he had ever seen. It seemed as big as a pony. Its mouth was wrinkled back in a terrible mirthless grin. The green light of its eyes pierced Meleager's chest like twin skewers. It was a cold night. The stones felt icy beneath his bare feet, but he was boiling inside. He had to have that noble beast for his own. The wonderful power pent in that lionlike shape was meant to serve him; he knew it was. The great heart that held such ferocity must be filled with passionate obedience to him, Meleager. This was to be *his* dog, the dog of dogs. The gods meant it so; that's why they had sent it.

He heard the animal snarl, a snarl that said death! Those huge jaws were about to tear out his throat. Across the darkness he could feel the whole body of the beast tensing to spring. He backed up, never taking his eyes off the dog, moving so swiftly and smoothly that he seemed to be sliding across the courtyard without moving his legs. Reaching behind him, he caught the edge of the kennel gate and pulled it open.

The dogs came pouring out, wild to attack, but he held them with a single word: "No!" They looked at him in bewilderment; they couldn't believe he was calling them back from attack, he, the beloved little figure who always led them in a pell-mell chase after their prey.

"No!" he said again. "Stand!"

They stood. But he could feel mounting force behind him, felt as if he were the frailest of dams holding back the mighty surge of a river in flood. And the simba hound, who had been prepared to leap, stood also, trying to understand. And what he understood was that he might kill that small morsel of a boy, but he'd never get to eat him—because those other dogs loved that boy. And they would fall upon him, the attacker, and tear him to pieces. For while he was larger and more powerful than any one of them, or any two, still these were big, fierce dogs and would be too many for him.

Nevertheless, he had never refused a fight in his life. He trembled with hunger and rage. Twenty pairs of eyes gleamed at him from behind the boy; as many sets of teeth flashed in the moonlight. Then, amazed, he saw the boy coming toward him. Heard him speak.

"You, big dog, accept me. We shall go hunting together. I shall show you such game as you have never known. See this splendid pack, finest hunters in all the world—well, you shall be their leader. You shall join your life to mine and we shall do nothing but hunt from morning till night. And what shall we pursue? Not merely meat on the hoof, but we shall know such sport as the gods enjoy. Killers we shall kill. Special creatures called monsters designed to be the bane of mortal man and mortal beast. These shall we bring to bay. For such have I been promised in my dreams—which also come from the gods. So stay, good dog. Let me come to you. Do not bite me."

Of course, the five-year-old Meleager could not say such words, nor could the great dog have understood them if they had been said. But Meleager, like all young heroes, was born with a magical lore that lived in his voice before he had the words for it. And the simba hound, like all great-hearted dogs, heard meanings in the human voice beyond what any words said.

So the child crossed the courtyard, walking toward the dog. Step by step his pack followed him. The simba hound growled low in his throat; the pack answered. Deep growling enwrapped the boy who was walking so slowly beneath the moon. He felt he was within a great vibrating bell. Danger bubbled in his blood. Made him smile. Made him laugh. He wanted to run across the courtyard now, and, risking all, fling his arms about that big furry neck.

He did not. He knew enough not to make any sudden move. He glided across the flagstones, the pack keeping pace.

Finally, boy and dog stood facing each other. Their heads were on a level. They stood eye to eye. Green fire mingled with hazel fire. But dogs judge by smell. And this boy cast a strange, joyous aroma: clean wood and goosefeathers of arrows, smell of running dog and lathered horse, cold scent of running water, and a fragrance of sunshine and crushed grass. The smell of the chase.

And the hungry dog wanted that chase to start immediately. The hot rage in his heart became a fire of comradeship. His hackles sank. He dipped his head, put an icy nose to the boy's face, then his hot tongue. Then indeed did Meleager fling his arms about the great furry neck, press his face to the dog's muzzle, and say, "I name you *Alcon*."

He whispered it into the simba hound's ear so that the others would not grow jealous. For *Alcon* meant mighty.

Lampon sat on a tree stump, thinking bitter thoughts as he waited for his brother. His leg was stretched straight before him;

Lampon sat on a tree stump, thinking bitter thoughts as he waited for his brother.

it was bandaged from ankle to knee. He felt that the birds in the trees were jeering at him. He heard someone approaching but didn't look up. He knew it was his brother and was too angry to look at him.

Plexippus spoke in a timid voice. "What's the matter with your leg?"

"Oh, nothing to trouble yourself about," said Lampon. "I'll just probably be lame for the rest of my life because of that damned dog."

"How could he do that? Weren't you wearing armor?"

"Indeed I was," said Lampon. "A full suit. It didn't seem to discourage him, though. He simply knocked me to the ground and tried to bite my leg off."

"He couldn't bite through brass. Don't tell me that."

"He closed those awful jaws about the brass greave covering my leg. He couldn't bite through, but he crushed the greave. Felt like he was pulping my shinbone. The smith needed a torch to cut me loose. Added a few burns to complete a charming evening."

"Well, things didn't turn out as we planned," murmured Plexippus.

"As *we* planned? Don't try to give me any credit for that plan. It was all yours, as you pointed out before we tried it. All yours, Brother, and it stank."

"Well, I'll simply think of something else," said Plexippus. "We're no worse off than we were before last night."

"Yes, we are," said Lampon. "At least I am. And as for our goal of taking over the kingdom, we're farther away than ever. It was bad enough that the king had assigned a special squadron of Royal Archers to protect the kid, but now we've helped out by providing him with a guardian worth three squadrons of Archers. That savage brute is utterly devoted to him and will rip anyone to pieces who even thinks an unkind thought about the brat."

"Things didn't turn out well, I admit it. Even the best generals lose a battle or two."

"But they occasionally win one."

"I'll find a way," said Plexippus. "I promise."

"That's a promise I seem to have heard before."

"Please, I'm studying the situation from every angle. Have a little patience."

"I've had nothing but patience," said Lampon. "We're not growing any younger, you know. I'd like to dip my hands into the royal treasury while I'm still young enough to enjoy it."

"Don't be ridiculous. We're still quite young, both of us. And very healthy."

"I was a lot healthier yesterday," said Lampon. "I had two legs."

"I'll make it up to you, brother. I'll give you that slave girl I took when we raided Lemnos last month. I've seen you looking at her."

"No, thanks," said Lampon. "She dresses her hair with rancid butter. Have you ever passed downwind of her?"

"Well, take your pick, then. I have a whole string."

"I know you do. I remember that raid. It was typical. While I was busy fighting, you were taking slaves."

"I'm offering you your pick, am I not?"

"Mmm. I might consider that blond Scythian."

"I was reserving her for my own use," said Plexippus. "But very well."

8

A Death and a Promise

For fifteen years boy and dog were inseparable. They hunted all over Calydon and into Arcadia and Aetolia. What they chased they caught; what they caught they killed. Bear, wolf, wild bull. They did not care to hunt any animal that could not put up a fight for itself.

When Meleager was nineteen, Alcon was fourteen, which is old for a hunting dog. He was as powerful as ever, but he had lost a lot of speed. The boy tried not to recognize this, but he knew that his dog had slowed down, and that he shouldn't be bringing big wild animals to bay. But when Meleager tried to go hunting without Alcon, the dog looked at him with such tragic eyes that he didn't have the heart to leave him behind.

"He's bound to get himself killed this way," said Meleager to himself. "But if I don't take him he'll die of grief. And I know he'd rather go out full of excitement and joy and battle fever. I know I would. I'd much rather die fighting."

So they continued to hunt together, the prince and the simba hound, and Meleager tried not to think what had to happen. Then one day it did happen.

They were chasing a gigantic bear up a hill. Meleager had

They continued to hunt together, the prince and the simba hound, and Meleager tried not to think what had to happen.

wounded him with an arrow, but the beast seemed to be climbing very easily. Finally, it turned, backed up against a rock, and stood at bay. And Alcon, as if knowing this to be a special day, appeared to regain the speed of his youth and rushed up the slope in a headlong charge as if he were chasing a doe instead of a bear. He left his feet, flew through the air straight for the bear's throat. The bear hunched its huge shoulder and swung its thick paw so fast it became a blur—batting the dog to the ground in mid-leap. Alcon sprang up immediately and closed his jaws on the bear's hind leg. Something he would not have done had he been able to reach higher. But he could not; his back was broken.

Meleager rushed up the slope, leveling his javelin. He did not dare throw it lest he hit his dog. Nor could he shoot arrows for the same reason. He was running as hard as he could but seemed to be going with agonizing slowness. For the bear was allowing the dog to bite one leg, while the great talons of his other paws were ripping Alcon to shreds.

By the time Meleager reached the spot, his beloved friend was a heap of bloody fur. Forgetting all about the bear, he stooped and gathered the dying dog in his arms. Alcon's green eyes looked into his. They were dulling now, but still held a spark of love.

By the time Meleager reached the spot, his beloved friend was a heap of bloody fur.

A warm tongue and cold nose touched his face for the last time. The great head lolled.

Then Meleager remembered the bear and sprang up, wild to kill. But the beast had sidled off. Meleager drew his sword; he meant to dig a grave. Then he shoved the sword back into its scabbard and lifted his face to the sky.

"No," he said. "I won't shut him away in a dark hole. Let him abide in the open air that he loved, under the wide sky and the sun and the moon and the stars. Let his bones be plucked clean by eagle and crow and carrion worm. Aye, let his brave bones whiten on the hillside; he shall be his own tomb. And shall live always in my memory as long as I myself live. And may the gods grant me as noble a death when my time comes."

From that time on Meleager haunted that range of hills, trying to find the bear that had killed his dog. But he could not. He sighted several bears; they were smaller, though, and he didn't bother chasing them.

His parents, the king and queen, were very worried about him. He would leave the castle at dawn and not come home until nightfall, and he looked so stricken by loss that his mother couldn't stand it. She had never wanted him to marry, had always feared the day when he would tell her that he had chosen a bride. But now, seeing him the way he was, she decided to speak to the king.

"I think our boy should marry," she said.

"I think our boy should marry," Queen Clymene said.

"Marry? Whom?"

"Anyone he chooses."

"Why, though? He's still very young."

"He needs something to make him happy—or someone. His heart is breaking because of that stupid dog."

"Nonsense!" said the king. "Hearts don't break so easily, and if they do, they mend themselves. Men die of sword thrust or spear thrust or well-aimed arrow. Or a bull gores them, perchance, or a bear claws them. But they do not die of grief. Only women do that, and not as often as they think."

Nevertheless, the king, who doted on his son almost as

much as his wife did, went to Meleager and said: "Perhaps it's time you married."

"Have anyone in mind?" said Meleager.

"No. But I thought you might. Calydon is famous for its beautiful girls."

"Father, please! I can't stand them. Soft, squealing little things, no good with spear or bow, hopeless on horseback. I'll not marry until I can find a girl who can hunt by my side."

"As you like, my son," said the king. "But remember this. We who are royal enjoy total privilege. One thing, however, are we not permitted—to appear downhearted. We may feel grief but not show it. For when kings weep, their tears water the seeds of fear and rage that are buried deep in the souls of those who are not kings, and these seeds ripen into revolt. You are heir to my throne, Meleager. If you would govern, smile—though your heart is breaking."

"Thank you, Father," said Meleager. "I shall not disappoint you."

He kissed his father's hand, then hurried out.

9

The Bear's Sister

eleager returned to the hills and hunted harder than ever, but with no luck. He kept hunting. Now he camped out instead of returning to the castle after dark, for some bears prowl by night.

Then, finally, he spotted a bear that looked big enough. He couldn't tell whether it was the one he wanted, but he thought it might be. It was gigantic.

The bear had seen him also. It stood halfway up the hill, looking down at him. Meleager tethered his horse well back among a fringe of trees, and started up the hill. He was surprised that the bear did not retreat. The huge beast seemed to be waiting for him, welcoming his attack. Anger flamed in Meleager. He made a great effort to control himself and advanced very cautiously.

The bear backed up a few steps, then wedged itself between two rocks, and waited there. The young man's hair whipped about his face, and he realized that a hard wind was blowing, a crosswind, that made him hesitate to use his bow. He could hope for no accuracy in such a wind, expert archer though he was. And to merely wound a beast that size would be worse than useless. It would not be weakened enough, and pain would feed its rage, making it even more dangerous.

Meleager danced about and shouted, trying to make the bear leave its shelter, trying to tempt it into charging downhill so that he might use the bear's own weight against it, meet the hurtling beast point-first, allowing it to impale itself upon his spear. The bear did not budge, just waited there between the two rocks. It uttered a chuckling growl that sounded to Meleager as though the beast were jeering at him. More than ever the prince was convinced that this was the bear that had killed his dog.

Forgetting all about caution, he charged up the hill straight at the rocks. The bear waited, and as soon as Meleager came within reach, swung its paw, knocking the spear out of his hand. It then charged so swiftly that the lad barely had time to draw his dagger before the beast was upon him. He saw the bear loom above him, stretch its enormous furry arms to catch him in a bone-crushing hug.

But to lift those heavy paws for the fatal embrace took slightly more time than if the bear had simply swung a paw knocking the youth to earth, or had raked him to shreds with its claws. Meleager was just able to slip under the outstretched paws, duck behind the bear, and sink his dagger into the back of its neck, but was knocked off his feet by its backward lurch. As he sprang up, he saw it rushing away up the slope, the dagger stuck in its neck. Blood was welling from the wound.

Meleager scrambled after it. Despite its terrible wound, the beast moved swiftly and was soon out of sight. Meleager followed the trail of blood, knowing that sooner or later the animal had to drop. It had been midmorning when he fought the bear; now the blazing summer sun was directly overhead, and he was panting as he ran.

Then, rounding a big boulder, he saw an astounding sight. A tall, bare-legged maiden was running down the hill with long strides. He gaped at her. She was wearing a great shaggy fur cloak. Just as he thought, "Why is she wearing that heavy thing

Meleager followed
the trail of blood. . .

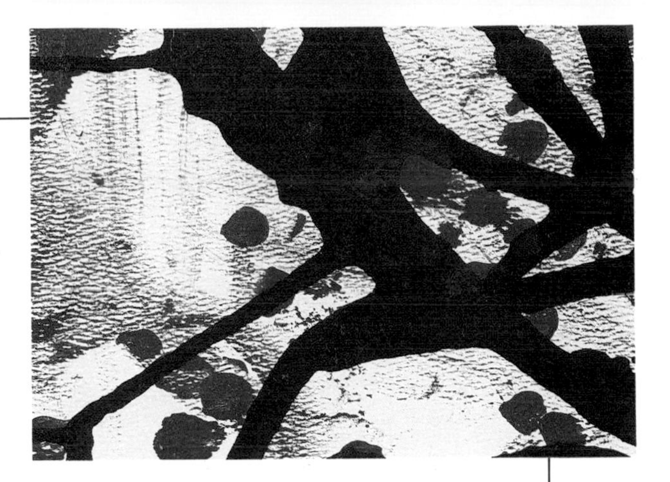

in all this heat?" he saw that blood was dripping on her shoulders, and realized that it was not a fur cloak she was wearing, but that she was carrying a huge bear on her back, the bear that he had fought.

The animal's head was lolling on her shoulder. Its blood was dripping all over her. He saw his dagger sticking out of its neck. He stood there, facing the girl. She stopped, let the bear slide to the ground, straightened up, and faced him. He was stunned by her beauty. Standing on long, sleek, powerful legs, she was as tall as he, perhaps taller. She was clad in a brief tunic of deerskin, her red-brown hair hanging to her thighs. Her face was muddy, her bare arms and shoulders streaked with blood.

He knew instantly that this was the one girl in the world for him.

"That's my bear," he said. "But I give him to you."

"Your bear?"

"My kill. That's my dagger, you know. I've been tracking him for hours, but you can—"

He was interrupted by her hoarse cry of rage. She stooped, scooped up a huge log as if it were a stick, and hurled it at his head. He ducked, felt it graze his hair. She bent again and pulled the dagger from the bear's neck. Then came slowly toward him.

"This bear is my brother," she said. "You have killed my brother. Now I shall kill you."

"Sweet maiden—"

"Sweet? I'm bitter as death, you'll find. Pick up your spear and fight."

*"I am Atalanta.
I belong to the clan
of mountain bears."*

He picked up his spear and threw it in the same motion. It cut through the air and split a sapling neatly in two. He turned and stood facing her with empty hands.

"You'll need a weapon," she said. "I mean to kill you."

"Come ahead. Try. Use the dagger if you like. It will make things more even."

She howled with fury and flung the dagger away. "Do me no favors," she cried. "I'll kill you with my hands."

She rushed at him. He caught her arms, trying to hold her back gently. It was impossible. She was as strong as a wild mare. She caught him in a great bear hug. He felt his ribs being crushed. Kicking, twisting, he broke her hold, then closed with her. There on the hillside, under a hot sun, before the dead eyes of the bear, they wrestled.

Atalanta was a powerful fighter. Adopted by a she-bear, she had grown up among bears, running with them, hunting with them, wrestling with them. She had grown into a gloriously tanned, supple young woman, strong as a she-bear herself. More than once she had taken a wild bull by its horns and twisted it off its hooves, so she was sure she could overcome Meleager easily. She planned to crush him in her hug and hurl him off the cliff.

However, as she wrestled with him under the sun, in the fragrance of trampled grass and pine needles, something new began to happen. As we know, when wrestling shaggy bears she had been puzzled that her own arms and legs seemed so smooth against their fur. She had wondered why she was so different, and didn't know whether she was glad or sorry. But now as she held the young man in her mighty hug, she felt his smoothness. It was as though she were holding herself—so that this body that was so strange to her was also wonderfully familiar. Trying to crush him in her arms, she found that she no longer knew where her body ended and his began. It seemed to her then that the fragrance of the trampled grass was rising in a sweet mist, robbing her of sense. She was dizzy. Her knees sagged. She, who could run up the side of a mountain, leaping from rock to rock, catching mountain goats in full stride . . . unbelievable to feel her legs weakening now. Her mind swooped and darkened and cast up a last thought.

"I am Meleager," he said. "I belong to you."

"It's magic. He's fighting me with magic . . ."

When her head cleared, she found they were sitting on the ground, their backs against an olive tree near the edge of the cliff, and looking onto a great scoop of blueness where a black hawk floated. Their arms were wrapped about each other's bodies as though they were still wrestling. She was telling her name.

"I am Atalanta. I belong to the clan of mountain bears."

"I am Meleager," he said. "I belong to you."

10

Two Jealousies

So the prince of Calydon found the mate he had dreamed of. They hunted together over hill and valley, through forest and field and swamp, on foot and on horseback—with dog pack or with long-legged Egyptian hunting cats called cheetahs. But more often they went out by themselves, for they preferred to be alone.

Plexippus was pleased by what was happening. He went to Lampon and said, "I have a plan, Brother."

"Another one? I hope it's better than the ones you've had before."

"It is. It is."

"I'm sure it is," said Lampon. "Your record is so bad that all you can do is improve."

"Do you want to hear it or not?"

"What's the difference? I'll hear it whether I want to or not."

"I'm setting no more physical traps for the lucky prince," said Plexippus. "All his life he's dwelt in the protection of his parents' love. But now, now I have the brilliant idea of turning that love against him. At least I'll turn his mother's, and she's more important in this matter than her husband."

"You're raving," cried Lampon. "Our sister dotes on her

son. Nothing you can say or do can turn her against him."

"It is her love itself that will curdle, I tell you. She has always been ready to be jealous of any girl he might want to marry. And I'm talking about eligible girls, heavily dowered, princesses and so forth. Imagine how she must feel about him wantoning around with this barefoot mountain slut. Well, I mean to fan the flames."

He left his brother and stalked off to find his sister. At first he chatted of this and that, Althea only half listening to him as was her habit. Then he said, "I heard an interesting tale, Sister. I heard that this new friend of Meleager belongs to a clan of mountain nymphs who hold to a very curious custom. It seems that they put their suitors through a courtship test. Each one of these nymphs demands of her suitor that he prove his love by cutting out his mother's heart and bringing it to her as a gift. I don't believe the tale, of course. But I thought it strange enough to tell it to you."

"Thank you," said Althea, and turned away. But he had caught the look in her eyes before her face was hidden by her hair. He strolled off, smiling to himself.

Althea nursed her grief in solitude. She knew how malicious her brother was, didn't really trust anything he said. Nevertheless, his words had found their mark. Her beloved son was tearing out her heart, if not literally with a knife, then by neglecting her for the sake of that wild wench from the hills. And Althea in her jealousy forgot that Meleager, who had been so sad after the death of his dog, now glowed with happiness. All she could think of was that her lovely boy had no thought for his mother anymore, only for that long-legged huntress.

As it happened, though, the beautiful couple had aroused the jealousy of someone more powerful than Althea. For the folk of Calydon who had glimpsed Atalanta and Meleager running across a field in the morning mist, or seen them silhouetted against the sunset, began to whisper that their prince had found a goddess

Artemis had always considered herself the fairest of the goddesses. . .

to be his mate. No one knew her name but it was certain she was a goddess, for she was as tall and strong and fleet as Artemis herself, and perhaps more beautiful.

These whispers drifted up to Artemis, Goddess of the Chase, Lady of the Silver Bow, and she burned with rage. She had always considered herself the fairest of the goddesses, more beautiful, in her own opinion, than Aphrodite, Goddess of Love and Beauty. Oh, yes, she far preferred her own lithe, suavely muscled figure to that of the lazy wide-hipped Aphrodite. And to have a mere human girl compared to her made her blaze with fury.

"I'll show them there's only one Artemis," she cried. "I'll send them such game as they'll never forget!"

And she whistled up the monstrous boar she had made of Stygian mud. Out of the steaming jungle of central Africa it came, trotted around the rim of North Africa, going west, then plunged into the waters of the Middle Sea and headed north toward Spain. As it swam it amused itself by killing a shark or two and mangling a few giant squid. It climbed ashore on the horn of Spain, galloped overland then, eastward to the great peninsula we now call Greece. And Artemis guided her monster pig through Euboea and Boeotia, through Mycenae, Achaea, and Arcadia, not letting it stop until it reached the lush hilly land called Calydon.

And the instructions she gave it then were, "Kill, kill, kill!"

11

The Monster

The monster boar immediately began to spread terror throughout the land. It uprooted trees, dug up crops, killed horses and cattle and those who tended them. It attacked men and women working in the fields, punching holes in them with its tusks, trampling them under its hooves until they were bloody rags. Nor was there any way to escape it when it was on a rampage, for it would hurtle into a house, knocking it to splinters, then kill everyone inside.

Shepherds and cowherds were afraid to graze their flocks, farmers refused to harvest their crops. So the people began to go hungry. The king didn't know what to do. He asked Meleager's advice. The young man was wild with excitement.

"Father, Father," he cried, "I'll kill the boar!"

"You alone?"

"Just I myself and one other."

"Are you mad?"

"We can do it, Father. We can kill any beast ever born."

"No, my son," said the king. "This is no ordinary boar. It's huge, incredibly strong, totally murderous. It's a monster. I'm afraid we have offended some god who has sent this beast to ravage the land. I don't understand it. I always sacrificed regularly to every one of the gods. Nevertheless, we have been cursed, and this dreadful beast roams the country, destroying, killing."

"I must hunt him, Father. This is the quarry we have dreamed of—something at last worthy of our skills."

"I forbid it," cried the king. "You are my only son. If you are killed, the throne will fall to your mother's idiot brothers, who will stuff into their pockets all that is left of my ravaged land. No, no, no, you shall not risk your life this way."

"The beast must be killed, Father. Or there will be no kingdom for you to rule or me to inherit."

"Yes, yes, we must contend with the monster, no doubt about that. But you shan't do it alone, or with that huntress of yours. We need a regular war party to go against the monster. What we shall do is invite all the best fighters in the lands of the Middle Sea to hunt the beast. They're all a little crazy like you, these heroes, and are always looking for a challenge. Well, they shall have one. It will be a famous affair."

"Call whom you like, Sire, but I shall lead the hunt," said Meleager.

Whereupon messages were sent to the greatest warriors of the Hellenic lands, inviting them to Calydon to hunt the giant boar. Those who weren't too busy killing each other accepted the invitation. Kings, princes, pirates, warlords, robber chieftains—they came flocking into Calydon.

The king was old now, however, and uneasy about playing host to so many rambunctious warriors. "I won't be able to go with them," he said to his wife. "Meleager will have to do the honors while I stay home to guard the castle."

"Why must you guard it?" said the queen. "Don't you trust your guests?"

"I trust them to act like themselves. They didn't become so rich in land and cattle by buying them, my dear. These men have always taken what they wanted. And may see in this enfeebled kingdom only a chance for booty."

"You must do what you think best," said the queen.

"I don't know what I think best. Sometimes I think this, sometimes that. I fear our guests as much as I do the boar—and yet my heart tells me my son may die on this hunt and that I should ride with him."

"You need not fear for our son," said Althea. "The Fates themselves permit me to guard his life."

"What fates? Where? How? What do you mean?"

Althea unlocked the great brass chest and lifted its lid. . .

Whereupon she told her husband how, upon the hour of Meleager's birth, she had been visited by Atropos, Lady of the Shears. Told him how the hag had thrown a stick into the fire. How she, Althea, had leaped from the bed to snatch it out of the flames. And how Atropos had promised that while the brand remained unburned the prince would not die.

"Do you expect me to believe this rigamarole?" cried the king. "Hags, sticks, promises. We can't risk our son's life on such nonsense."

"Be careful what you call nonsense," said Althea. "You're in enough trouble now without offending the eldest Fate."

"Prove that it's not nonsense."

"Behold!" cried Althea.

She unlocked the great brass chest, lifted its lid, and showed him the charred stick.

The king was still inclined to disbelieve, but looking at the blackened branch and studying his wife's face, he knew that she was speaking the truth.

"I see," he muttered.

"So set your mind at rest, dear husband. Let him lead the hunt while you stay here and guard the castle. Besides, I'm sending my brothers to keep an eye on him."

"Who'll keep an eye on them?"

"Stop it, please," said the queen. "I know your opinion of my brothers, but they'll be more careful than you about certain matters. They'll carry out my wishes and prevent him from bringing that wild hussy of his to join the hunt."

"You're very wrong to interfere," said the king. "Meleager loves that girl and will never love another."

"Love, love, what does he know about love, that stripling with his mother's milk scarcely dry on his lips? I tell you that he shall never bring her home as his wife, not while I draw breath."

"Well, I can't worry about that at the moment," said the king. "I have heavier things on my mind. Monstrous beasts, fearsome guests—the wild girl will have to wait."

"She'll wait long before she marries my son," said Althea.

Early the next morning, everyone gathered for the hunt. The guests were astounded when Meleager rode up with Atalanta at his side. They goggled in wonder at the lovely, lithe young huntress who sat a great grey horse. She was clad in a deerskin tunic, wore bow and quiver, and held a javelin. All of them were surprised, some of them were angered at the thought that Meleager was taking the hunt lightly, and some younger ones were inflamed by her beauty and growing jealous of Meleager.

The couple sat their horses solidly. Meleager was stone faced, Atalanta smiling. The prince's uncles rode toward him.

"You're disgracing us," croaked Plexippus. "And dishonoring our noble guests. They do not wish to ride out with this bear's whelp from the hills."

Meleager touched his horse with his heels, walked it between his uncles' horses, and grasped an arm of each—squeezing

Early the next morning, everyone gathered for the hunt.

them until they felt their elbows cracking in his iron grip.

"One more insulting word out of you," he whispered, "and I'll call off this hunt and send everyone away. And Atalanta and I will hunt the boar alone, as we have always wished. But first, I will smash your heads together so that our guests may see where the fault lies."

The uncles were silent. Meleager lifted his horn and sounded a call that rang through the hills. Laughing, shouting, arms glittering, the company rode forth to hunt the boar.

They did not ride far. The boar came to meet them. It selected its position very cannily, choosing a canyon where the walls narrowed so that it could be attacked only from the front and by no more than two men at a time.

But these were expert hunters. Meleager did not have to guide them by hand signals. They knew what to do. They did not rush in to attack, but strung themselves out before the mouth of the canyon. They pranced and shouted, clashed spear against shield, trying to excite the boar so that it would charge out of the canyon.

It did not.

They advanced, shouted more loudly, beat their shields harder. No movement from the boar. The uncles had not advanced. They had reined up their horses well away from the canyon and were watching from afar.

The men were losing their caution now. They advanced to within a spear's throw of the canyon mouth. Then, although the beast was half-hidden in a tangle of brush, they sent a flight of arrows into its hiding place. They were determined to draw the beast out. It was simply too dangerous to go into that narrow cleft after it. They came closer and sent another flight of arrows into the brush.

This time they succeeded, and their success was a disaster. They had underestimated the monster's size and speed. It came. It came hurtling out of the canyon with the crushing force of a boulder rolling down a mountain side. It charged into a party of hunters, scattering them in all directions, then whirled lightly as a panther, trampling two of the men to bloody shreds under its razor hooves.

The boar charged into a party of hunters . . . trampling two of the men to bloody shreds under its razor hooves.

The hunters fled; the boar followed. It caught two of them, spearing one with its tusk and shearing his leg off at the hip. Two warrior brothers, Telamon, who became the father of Ajax, and Peleus, who was to become the father of Achilles, showed their enormous courage by walking slowly in on the boar, spears outthrust. Their example inspired others to form a ragged circle about the boar.

But the beast charged Telamon, breaking through a hedge of spears. Peleus flung his javelin. It skidded off the boar's shoulder and pierced one of the hunters, who fell dead. Another man swung his battle-axe at the boar; it tilted its head, parrying the axe—then with a savage counterthrust ripped out the man's belly, gutting him like a fish.

The beast then charged Peleus, who would have died on the spot, leaving no son named Achilles—and Hector might have lived and Troy stood unburned—but Atalanta drew her bow and loosed a shaft into the unprotected spot behind the boar's ear. The arrow sank in up to its feathers. Any other animal would have been killed instantly, but the boar still lived, and seemed as strong as ever, murderously strong.

Howling with pain, it chased Atalanta. She did not flee. She notched another arrow and stood facing the beast as it rushed toward her. There was just enough time for her to send an arrow into its eye. But it kept hurtling toward her.

Meleager, shouting a war cry, flung himself right into the boar's path, hurling a javelin as he ran. It sank into the boar, under its shoulder, turning it from its course.

Now it rushed toward Meleager, who kept running toward it and leaped clear over the charging beast like a Cretan bull dancer. He landed behind it. Before the boar could turn, he swung his sword in a glittering arc, slashing under the great hump of muscle, cutting the spinal cord. The massive low-slung body tottered, tilted, fell. Even that incarnation of monstrous energy could not live after the cable of its life was cut.

Meleager, shouting a war cry, flung himself right into the boar's path. . .

The boar lay dead.

A great cheer went up from the bloody, battered crowd of hunters. Meleager nodded at them, pulled out his knife, knelt at the side of the giant carcass and calmly began to skin it. When he was finished he came to Atalanta with the pelt in his arms. He bowed and said:

"Your arrow struck first. The hide belongs to you."

Now this boar hide made a priceless gift. It was so tough that it made a wonderful flexible battle garment, lighter and stronger than armor, able to turn wolf bite, spear thrust, flying arrow.

Plexippus, who had hung back from the actual fighting and

hadn't come anywhere near the boar, sensed that the other hunters might resent Meleager giving this splendid trophy to the girl, and decided to take advantage of this resentment. He rode toward Meleager, beard bristling. Lampon joined him.

"What kind of hospitality is this, O Nephew?" he cried. "It would be unprincely, of course, for you to claim the hide for yourself though you killed the boar, but the least you can do is offer it to one of your distinguished guests."

Then he turned upon Atalanta, spittle flying from his lips as he berated her. "And you, you're a vile witch. You have cast an enchantment upon this poor lad. His wits are addled; he doesn't know what he's doing. Give that hide back, instantly—or you'll regret it."

Meleager was listening quietly. He wiped the blood from his sword with a handful of dry grass, studied the gleaming blade, then swung it twice. The heads of his uncles fell in the dust, so quickly parted from their necks that they still seemed to be cursing as they fell. The guests were stunned. Meleager turned to them, and said:

"I beg you, sirs, to pardon this unpleasant family brawl. However, if any of you, perchance, feels too much offended, I shall be glad to measure swords with him. If not, you are all invited to the castle to a feast celebrating the death of the boar and honoring the fair huntress, Atalanta, whom I intend to make my wife."

The hunters raised a great shout. Some of them may have been angry, others jealous, but they all admired courage whenever it showed itself. Besides, none of them were too eager to fight Meleager; they had seen him in action. So they all rode toward the castle, all but Atalanta and Meleager, who excused themselves and rode off to be alone for a few hours before the festivities began.

When the hunters reached the castle they were met by the

king and queen who eagerly demanded to hear their tale. Peleus, who was their spokesman more or less, told of the fight with the boar, how some of the party had been killed, others wounded. How Atalanta had shot an arrow into the boar, drawing first blood, and would have been killed herself had not Meleager rushed into the beast's path and slain it with his sword.

But when it was told how Meleager had presented the boar's hide to Atalanta, how his uncles had protested, and been beheaded for their trouble, then the queen went white with fury and left the room. She went to her chamber and sank to her knees on the stone floor that was covered by the skins of the animals Meleager had slain—wolfskin, bearskin. She had always trod them with pleasure because he had given them to her.

She tried to picture Meleager's face, tried to remember how much she loved him, for she was shocked by her own feelings, could not believe the intention that was forming within her. "No. no," she cried, "I love him. I love him."

Then she heard her brother's voice, saying: "Curious tale of these mountain nymphs. Seems that before one of them will accept a suitor he has to cut out his mother's heart and bring it to her as a gift."

Althea walked on her knees to the brass chest, leaned her arms upon it and buried her face in her arms, sobbing. "Bad prince, cruelest of sons, you have sent my two brothers to Tartarus, and in their stead propose to bring home this wild nymph of the hills. It shall not be, my son, my enemy. The Lady of the Shears has given your mother the power to prevent you."

Mad with grief, Althea flung open the brass chest. She pulled the charred stick from its place and threw it on the fire, and watched it burn.

While this was happening, Meleager and Atalanta were in their favorite place under the twisted olive tree on the cliff, looking out into a great blue gulf of space.

"I want to be your wife," murmured Atalanta. "You're the

Plexippus sensed that the other hunters might resent Meleager giving this splendid trophy to the girl. . .

only one I have ever loved or ever shall love. But, my dearest, I don't want to live in a castle. I don't want to be a queen and wear dresses and sit on a throne. Why can't we stay the way we are, roaming the hills, hunting, fighting? Oh, can't we?"

Meleager uttered a scalding cry of agony as his hair caught fire.

"We will, we will!" cried Meleager. "King and queen we must be. But for every day we spend indoors sitting on thrones, making laws and so forth, for every day spent so poorly, I promise you that we shall spend ten days riding, hunting, fighting . . . you and I together, side by side. This is my solemn vow, Atalanta—Atalanta, my lovely one—and this I swear, too—"

She heard his voice stop. She saw him clutch his chest. Saw his eyes bulge, his face go purple. She caught him in her arms. His head snapped back. His scorched lips parted. He uttered a scalding cry of agony as his hair caught fire. She tried to bat out the flames, but only burned her hands. And it was no use. He was dead. His charred body smoldered on the grass.

In the castle, Queen Althea scattered the ashes of the burnt stick with her foot, stamping out the last spark. Then she straightened her robes, combed her hair with a silver comb, and went down to tend to her guests.

But the moon goddess, for all her power, had failed. Her boar was dead while her rival still lived. And although Atalanta wished she had died with Meleager, life ran too richly in the tall girl for her to kill herself. She left Calydon and went back to Arcadia where she had been born. And wherever she went, legend attended her.

Poseidon, it is told, glimpsed her running along the shore one day, fell violently in love with her, and gave her name to his most important ocean. And Artemis, whose jealousy has not cooled after all these thousands of years, still instructs her moon to swing the Atlantic tides very roughly, making it the most feared of all the seas.

Acknowledgments

Letter Cap Illustrations by Hrana L. Janto

Cover, THE CALYDONIAN BOAR *(1988) by Emilio Cruz, oil on paper (37 × 48")*
Courtesy of the artist
Photo: Karen Bell

Opposite page 1, BOAR NO. 2 *(1988) by Earl Staley, acrylic on canvas (8 × 10")*
Courtesy of the artist
Photo: Karen Bell

Page 3, DIANA SEATED ON A STAG *(early 18th century, German Automaton: silver, silver-gilt, jewels, and enamel (14 3/4 × 9 1/2")*
Courtesy of the Metropolitan Museum of Art, gift of J. Pierpont Morgan, 1917 (17.190.746)

Page 5, NIGHT MIST *by Jackson Pollock (1912–1956), oil on canvas (91.4 × 187.9 cm.)*
Courtesy of the Collection Norton Gallery of Art, West Palm Beach
Photo: Art Resource, NY

Page 7, BONESCAPE *(1986) by Emilio Cruz, oil on canvas (7 × 7')*
Courtesy of the Artist

Page 8, MONSTER (FOR CHARLES IVES) *(1959) by Robert Motherwell, oil on canvas (198 × 200 cm.)*
Courtesy of the National Museum of Art, Washington, D.C.
Photo: Art Resource, NY

Page 10, MIST IN KANAB CANYON, UTAH *by Thomas Moran (1837–1926), oil on canvas*
Courtesy of the National Gallery, Washington, D.C.
Photo: Art Resource, NY

Page 13, WOMAN OF THE VELCHA FAMILY *(ca. 470 B.C.), Etruscan fresco from the tomb of Orcus*
Photo: Art Resource, NY

Page 14, RHEA PRESENTING A STONE IN THE FORM OF A BABY TO KRONOS *(5th century B.C.), Greek red-figured attic vase (h. 13 11/16")*
Courtesy of the Metropolitan Museum of Art, Rogers Fund, 1906 (06.1021.144 Side A)

Page 16, HEAD OF A BABY BY ANDREA DEL SARTO *(1486–1530), pen and ink and chalk on paper*
Courtesy of Gabinetto Disegni, Florence
Photo: Scala/Art Resource, NY

Page 18, STAG AND DOE *(late 14th century) by Giovanni de Grassi, pen and ink and watercolor on paper*
Courtesy of Biblioteca Civica, Bergamo

Page 19, BEAR, *etching by Stefano della Bella (1610–1664)*
Courtesy of the Metropolitan Museum of Art, Purchase, Joseph Pulitzer Bequest, 1917 (17.50.17.253)

Page 20, WITH SLOPING MAST AND DIPPING PROW *by Albert Pinkham Ryder (1847–1917), oil on canvas*
Courtesy of the National Museum of American Art, Washington, D.C.
Photo: Art Resource, NY

Page 22, THE FISHERMAN *(ca. 1500 B.C.), fresco from Akrotiri, Thera.*
Photo: Art Resource, NY

Page 25, CHILD IN ITS MOTHER'S ARMS, LOOKING AT HER INTENSELY *by Mary Cassatt (1844–1926), oil on canvas*
Courtesy of the Collection Phillipe Roy, Maurecourt
Photo: Giraudon/Art Resource, NY

Page 27, HAUNTED EVENING *by Charles Burchfield (1893–1967), watercolor on paper*
Photo: Art Resource, NY

Page 30, CAPE SPLIT *by John Marin (1870–1953), oil on canvas*
Photo: Art Resource, NY

Page 32, LES VIEILLES, *detail by Francisco Goya (1746–1828), oil on canvas*
Courtesy of the Musée des Beaux Arts de Lille, Jardin du Musée, Lille
Photo: Giraudon/Art Resource, NY

Page 34, NIÑO *by Diego Rivera (1886–1957), tempera with oil resins on masonite*
Courtesy of Sotheby Parke-Bernet
Photo: Art Resource, NY

Page 36, PORTRAIT OF A BOY *(early 3rd century B.C.), Etruscan bronze (h. 9")*
Courtesy of the Archaeology Museum, Florence
Photo: Art Resource, NY

Page 39, BEGINNING OF THE WAR *(ca. 380 B.C.), Etruscan tomb fresco*
Courtesy of the Paestum Museum
Photo: Scala/Art Resource, NY

Page 42, DOGS ON A TILE FLOOR *(1986) by Heidi Endemann, watercolor and gold leaf on paper (42 × 32 1/2")*
Courtesy of Alexander F. Milliken Inc., NY

Page 44, DOG IN A THICKET, *detail from a Franco-Flemish tapestry,* THE HUNT OF THE UNICORN *(ca. 1500), silk, wool, silver, and silver-gilt thread (12' 1" × 13' 2")*
Courtesy of the Metropolitan Museum of Art, The Cloisters Collection, Gift of John D. Rockefeller, Jr., 1937 (37.80.4)

Page 48, PORTRAIT OF A MAN *(3rd century), Roman floor mosaic*
Courtesy of the Museo Gregoriano, Vatican
Photo: Art Resource, NY

Page 50, BRONZE STATUE FROM THE SEA OF MARATHON *(4th century B.C.)*
Courtesy of the National Museum, Athens
Photo: Nimatallah/Art Resource, NY

Page 52, STAG HUNT *(380 B.C.), Etruscan fresco*
Courtesy of the Paestum Museum
Photo: Scala/Art Resource, NY

Page 53, LAST FOOTHOLD *(1987) by Sylvia Glass, acrylic-pastel on cloth (51 × 48")*
Courtesy of Harcourts Contemporary, San Francisco

Page 54, THE LADY OF ELCHE *(5th century B.C.)*
Courtesy of the Iberian Archaeology Museum
Photo: Scala/Art Resource

Page 56, STANDING BEAR *by Antoine Louis Barye (1796–1875), bronze (h. 9 5/8")*
Courtesy of the Graham Gallery, NY

Page 59, RED STORM *(1980) by Mark Willis, acrylic and black India ink on paper (4 3/4 × 6 5/8")*
Courtesy of the artist
Photo: Karen Bell

Page 60, GREEK BOX MIRROR WITH THE HEAD OF A WOMAN *(4th century B.C.), bronze (diameter 6 1/8")*
Courtesy of the Metropolitan Museum of Art, Rogers Fund, 1907 (07.256ab)

Page 61, BOX MIRROR WITH THE HEAD OF PAN *(4th century B.C.), Greek metalwork—bronze (diameter 6 3/4")*
Courtesy of the Metropolitan Museum of Art, Fletcher Fund (25.78.44a–d)

Page 62, THE STORM *by Pierre Auguste Cot (1837–1883), oil on canvas (92 1/4 × 61 3/4")*
Courtesy of the Metropolitan Museum of Art, Bequest of Catherine Lorillard Wolfe Collection, 1887 (87.15.134)

Page 65, DIANA OF GABIES, *marble copy of original by Praxiteles (370–330 B.C.)*
Courtesy of the Louvre, Paris
Photo: Art Resource, NY

Page 66, THE BOAR FROM HELL *(1988) by Emilio Cruz, oil on paper (37 × 48")*
Courtesy of the artist
Photo: Karen Bell

Page 69, PERSEPHONE OPENS A CHEST *(ca. 4th century B.C.), sculptural relief*
Courtesy of the National Museum of Archaeology, Reggio Calabria
Photo: Scala/Art Resource, NY

Page 71, THE HUNT *(1935) by Corrado Gagli, oil on canvas*
Courtesy of the Pecci Blunt Collection, Marlia
Photo: Scala/Art Resource, NY

Page 72, THE HUNT OF THE CALYDONIAN BOAR *(ca. 575–550 B.C.), detail from* THE FRANÇOIS VASE
Courtesy of the Archaeology Museum, Florence
Photo: Scala/Art Resource, NY

Page 74, STORY OF ADONIS/BOAR HUNT *(1982) by Earl Staley, acrylic on canvas (52 × 85")*
Courtesy of the artist

Page 77, MELEAGER AND ATALANTA *by Jacob Jordaens (1593–1678), oil on canvas*
Photo: Kavaler/Art Resource, NY

Page 78, MAN WITH FLAMING HAIR, NO. 2 *(1988) by Earl Staley, acrylic on canvas (8 × 10")*
Courtesy of the artist
Photo: Karen Bell

BOOKS BY BERNARD EVSLIN

Merchants of Venus
Heroes, Gods and Monsters of the Greek Myths
Greeks Bearing Gifts: The Epics of Achilles and Ulysses
The Dolphin Rider
Gods, Demigods and Demons
The Green Hero
Heraclea
Signs & Wonders: Tales of the Old Testament